False Equivalents

Dispatches from an Angst-Ridden Land

False Equivalents

Dispatches from an Angst-Ridden Land

Jack Homer

False Equivalents: Dispatches from an Angst-Ridden Land

Jack Homer

"Jeff's World" previously appeared in *Mobius, The Journal of Social Change,* Spring 2021, Volume 32, Number 1.

Cover image: "Ceci n'est pas une pipe" (after Magritte) by Carlos Barberena (carlosbarberena.com).

ISBN-13: 979-8715632791
ISBN-10: 8715632791

CONTENTS

Logging out (Hadlock Lake)   1

Pre-mortem post-mortem   3

Now, alphabetized   6

We are not like this   8

Orchiectomy   10

Stumped   12

Stone chutney   14

First responder   16

Shot in black and white (MLK/FBI)   18

It got so real   20

Jeff's world   22

Regression to the mean   26

Logging out (Hadlock Lake)

Lakeside deck, breeze, lapping water,

the weekend over, most have left but we stay on;

calmer now but for a distant chainsaw

and the dog worrying at his tie-line,

grumbling over his shackled state.

End of summer, goldenrod, the new sneezing season

announces itself with itchy eyes and aggravated brain;

drained of clarity, purposeless,

I become a limp sock puppet

with one eye missing and the other hanging loose,

ego shredded like so much moo-shu.

Again we catch the sorry glimpses

of summer camp half a century ago,

when I was the one who hesitated

walking across the log above the rocky stream;

no problem, my counselor urged, you can do it,

but still I lost my balance and fell.

The lake, the dog, the sock, the log,

All seen in a smudged rearview mirror;

but don't worry, it's just a temporary fog—

at some point it clears,

revealing a blinding blue expanse.

August 2016

Pre-mortem post-mortem

In light of the dark decision

And the darker days surely to come,

How are we to begin anew our small daily tasks

And the courtesies and kindnesses meant to make things better,

Done from the heart and the knowledge of common destiny?

Let's start by calling out that certain distance

That goes with the accomplished position,

The social status achieved.

You will find it there in your colleagues and friends, and

If you look closely, you will find it there in yourself.

But wait, haven't we always tried our best and

Done what we were supposed to do?

As to those losers, those ignorant hicks,

Don't they just bring it on themselves,

And then complain that they've been screwed?

And when we try to help them,

They bite the hand that feeds.

So, really now, what do we owe them?

How can we be blamed?

There is truth in this argument,

And as a believer in truth,

I've made it many times myself.

But there is also self-deception:

We do not want to deal with those people,

And we insist that they see the light, our light,

Or else keep their distance.

So now they tell us they will not see our light

And will not keep their distance.

They will not acknowledge their contradictions,

And will brazenly deny the facts

Upon which our civilized world is constructed.

How can one speak of a working democracy

And the genius of the people

When the people have become so degraded,

Their minds filled with vituperative nonsense?

Well, we must try, harder than we have done so far.

We must try even if at first we recoil

As if from dust-encrusted crawling creatures,

Yes, even if they are rough and as mean as snakes.

Let us also hang our heads a little

And admit we did not understand "common destiny" correctly.

We assumed it was about progress and evolution,

With those rough creatures dying out as their children

Flew the coop and excelled.

No, this is not Europe nor is it Canada.

It is a rougher place that is proud of its roughness

And keeps its home-schooled children close to home.

As inner-city poverty can be self-perpetuating,

So can back-country snake rattling.

We don't have the option of just wishing it away.

November 2016

Now, alphabetized

Acid

Baiting

Bankrupt

Broiling

Climactic

Conditioned

Conspiratorial

Corrupt

Desperate

Far-fetched

Far-reaching

Fear-mongering

Hateful

Imaginary

Indigestible

Ineffable

Inevitable

Insane

Irreducible

Lemming-like

Marching

Mendacious

Misanthropic

Mob-inciting

Normalized

Pan-fried

Petrified

Post-democratic

Power-hungry

Pre-apocalyptic

Predisposed

Stalking

Stomping

Threatening

Unaffordable

Unconscionable

Unwatchable

Vice-gripped

Wasted

Wiped

July 2018

We are not like this

When we say resist, what are we resisting?

We need to be clear we are resisting the whole circle of evil,

The whole fucking kit and kaboodle.

If you enjoyed the back-stabbing and casual cruelty of The Apprentice,

Or of Survivor, or of the Kardashians,

You are complicit.

You demanded civility and restraint but lacked it yourself.

You connived and tore up the rules.

You denied Merrick Garland with a smirk on your face.

You enriched the fortunate and shackled the poor.

You tore families apart and said they deserved it.

You bought the guns that killed all the innocents.

You bought a gas-guzzling truck and burned up the sky.

You turned our civilization upside down and didn't give a shit.

Mostly, you allowed your humanity to be stolen

By Fox and Friends

By online werewolves

By those who embrace greed

And are so obviously perverse and cruel.

You were whupped or spoiled as a child and were taught tit-for-tat,

And now you preach tit-for-tat to the world.

You reduce everything to survival of the fittest

And believe only in strength and submission.

You are angry at those around you,

Have killing and maiming on your rat-a-tat mind,

And you don't know why.

I am not like this.

My friends are not like this.

Most people are not like this.

But many are, victims of evil and become evil themselves.

We must see them for what they have become,

Understand they have temporarily gained the upper hand,

And, though it is a role we adopt reluctantly,

Resist them at every turn.

August 2018

Orchiectomy

Here sits the killer whale, the orca, aye-aye,

Two weeks after excision of the starboard testicle.

And there, by gar, is his human counterpart,

Signor Deflato, the pirate,

Former master of the seas,

Finding it hard to sit still for long,

Seized up inside and walking the plank,

His baggy eyes covered by a bloody blindfold.

Ancient animal, ancient mariner,

Both need the rush of action,

Else drag them leeward, land ho,

Put out to pasture

Under a picturesque headstone on the hill.

Will whale and pirate rise again?

Can they overlook the gouging

That has rendered the wrinkled flesh and the sagging spirit?

Can they move on to delight again in the waves

In spite of their weeping wounds?

No one understands the will of a whale,

Nor that of the pirate backing off the plank

Stepping back into the frigate, his hairy heart intact;

Stumbling over to the portside deck

To salute his blubbery nemesis

And to begin (shouting hell with them all) again.

February 2019

Stumped

Shut in for months and ground up inside.

There are no grounds for complaint

In a rural hamlet,

But all us piggies are oinking to be let loose.

The garden is watered, the trees are thriving,

And we're hunkered down in a watering hole for two.

Hanging out with the dog, watching the birds or the river,

Zooming or streaming with our eyes bulging and sore heads pulsing.

Sore with each other for no reason other than proximity,

Because piggies are naturally grouchy when penned in, though some deny it.

What changed? Why so glum, chum?

I've always worked from home, no big deal.

She was ready for retirement, bring it on.

We like spending lots of time at home.

But we do not sleep well, and we're dying to get out.

Though we don't want to die, not yet,

And surely not until after the mafia Don is Drumpfed out of office.

The world will keep burning, we know that,

But we yearn for the pleasure of that Drumpfing.

Last year we took down two tall dying pines by the book-cabin out back.

We truncated them. We had their stumps ground down to the dirt.

This was the right thing to do and it made us feel better.

But it did not make us any younger,

And now we are the stumped ones.

August 2020

Stone chutney

My Eve in the garden

brings pears picked from the old tree,

a tree that was here before we were.

We must snare the pears before

they fall to the ground,

clanging off the tin roof of the shed

in their descent to the soil,

soon chomped by the greedy deer.

Eve has claimed a paltry few,

spotted, uneven, and hard

sitting in the little terracotta bowl

trying to ripen on the warm back porch

of late summer.

Not so great eaten whole, she says,

but maybe we could make pear chutney—

still, even a week later, they remain hard as rocks.

Ten summers have passed in our little yellow house,

and the tree has never produced pliant fruit.

Let's face it, I say, it's a crappy old tree

(despite its numerical bounty and craggy good looks,

providing sustenance and shade

to the does and their wobbly spotted fawns,

appreciated by our porch pooch and other sunset spectators)—

of limited usefulness to fancy country folks like us

looking for finer fare.

October 2020

First responder

Big guy here at the counter, awfully drunk

Just tried to pass a fake 20

For a pack of cigs.

I told him give it back, but he won't.

Probably high, too.

Said he's a security guard here weekends

Moved up here for a better life.

Can you believe that drivel?

Better get here quick.

Show your hands, fucker, show your hands.

Hey, Derek, that you? Remember me?

We overlap shifts sometimes?

Shut up, fucker, I don't know you.

You high on something?

No, just scared, officer.

Guys, I need some backup here,

I got the big man down but he's a crazy one.

Please, officer, I can't breathe,

You don't have to do this,

Everything hurts,

Mama,

I can't breathe, Mama,

I can't breathe.

January 2021

Shot in black and white (MLK/FBI)

How many times did he walk down those roads,

leaning against the blowing wind?

Honored in his time by the Nobel committee but

called a man by only 17% of his own country,

while the white lizard, the hoover,

sucked up dirt and weaponized it in manila piles,

to bend the nation to his will,

looked straight into the TV camera, inverting reality,

until most considered him the greater patriot,

while he failed to protect the walking man.

More than 50 years have passed,

but the lizard's poison has not,

and even those who should know better,

who have faced oppression themselves,

allow a double standard to persist,

sell their soul for a piece of celebrity pie,

coopted by contemptible squawking heads,

hoodwinked into innuendos and ambivalences.

The lizard's white hood is still in our midst,

its wearer winking and spreading the lie,

a lie lapped up by millions of small minds,

ready to believe, ready to believe,

a return to the good old days.

How many times down these filthy old roads?

January 2021

It got so real

We watched them down there getting real

Really real, and so freaking beautiful I tell you.

We felt so proud they were standing up for us real folks

Moving forward smashing the barricades to our freedom

Because we've been down so long but now it's our turn.

Now, I know he lives at home with me

And hasn't made much of himself before now

But he sure is good on that computer and

Has made a lot of online friends.

His self-esteem seems good now, too,

And he's trying hard to cut back on

All that fooling around he did before.

Really hard.

What a good son

Now that he's turned his passion to something

So real and, like, important for all of us here

Who never get a fair shake from life.

I'm not going to complain too much

But we deserve better.

Those hot shots just kept putting us down,

Putting us down until we couldn't take it no more.

Don't you cancel me, don't you dare cancel me.

I'm real, and I won't be cancelled. Ever.

January 2021

Jeff's world

"QAnon promoters have in the past day held up an incoherent set of new theories to explain away Trump's anticlimactic exit from Washington: that the military is in control of the country, not Biden; that Biden and Trump have switched faces; that Biden's inauguration was illegitimate, and that the real one (for Trump) would take place in March; or that Biden has been in on the QAnon plan all along."
- Drew Harwell, Washington Post, 1/21/2021

He was a good friend in junior high,

A smart kid with a sly sense of humor,

And a rung above me on the chess team.

We lived in different neighborhoods;

I never saw his home and he never saw mine.

We went to different high schools

But stayed in touch somewhat.

Before joining the Army,

He changed his last name

To one that sounded less Jewish.

Some people did that, I guess,

Even in the seventies.

He wrote me from Germany,

Where he was stationed,

A mainstay on the Army chess team,

Competing all around Europe, he said.

The Army paid for his college education,

And he became a high school science teacher

Back in the southern California suburbs

Where we had grown up.

We lost touch for 20 years

Until Facebook came along and he found me.

He'd grown a full beard

And supplemented his teaching income

By selling original fractal art online.

Higher mathematics, Mandelbrot sets.

A solid six figures a year, he said.

Another 20 years passed,

And he was pleased to announce his retirement from teaching.

Maybe I congratulated him, I'm not sure.

I didn't really look at Facebook much anymore,

And didn't know anything about who he was now.

I figured he was an upstanding guy,

Who had done a good thing, a noble thing,

By sticking with the Valley, our home,

Although it had become different over time,

Much more diverse, majority Hispanic.

It must have started sometime during 2020.

An increasing number of Facebook posts,

More than I'd ever seen him write before.

The subject lines appeared innocuous,

Announcing new photos and the like,

And I deleted them without looking.

But then, after the Inauguration,

A subject line I couldn't ignore,

An apology from Jeff

To all of his followers and friends.

It was hard to make out the meaning,

And I had to read it several times

To understand that he was apologizing

For predicting previously

That the evil Democrats,

That cesspit of corruption and pedophilia,

Could never take the White House,

That the patriots of our nation and God

Would never allow that to happen.

I'm sorry, he said, I didn't realize

This country was so much in God's disfavor.

From chess to fractals

To the depths of conspiracy

His Army goes marching on

Reveling in the beautiful logic of His Creation.

January 2021

Regression to the mean

It's so challenging

this idea of social change when

we take one step forward

and then are shoved back down the stairs

by the self-proclaimed patriots

who believe we need protection from change.

They used to be known for their hospitality

and simple virtue and kindness

but they were hypnotized

by the bubbling-hot blabbermouths

who insist that their setbacks can be traced

to outsiders and nanny-state elites.

It does not matter to the angry mob that

this zero-sum news is a demonstrable lie

and that openness and tolerance

have always been our sauce of success--

our only valid claim to being a special place

and the very thing that lifted up

their own great-grandparents in this country.

We have seen in smashed glass and smeared feces

how they would now rather destroy

and die if necessary

than respect the will of a majority

who try to tell them to calm down and be civil.

I read that 90 percent of white evangelicals

(proud of their adherence to Scripture)

say that Scripture has no bearing on

how they think about immigration policy.

Perhaps their new Scripture has Jesus saying

that the mean shall inherit the Earth.

February 2021

9 798715 632791